Harvard University

The Rules and By-Laws of the Board of Overseers of Harvard

College

Vol. 1

Harvard University

The Rules and By-Laws of the Board of Overseers of Harvard College
Vol. 1

ISBN/EAN: 9783337811686

Printed in Europe, USA, Canada, Australia, Japan

Cover: Foto ©Suzi / pixelio.de

More available books at **www.hansebooks.com**

THE

RULES AND BY-LAWS

OF THE

Board of Overseers of Harvard College;

TO WHICH IS APPENDED

THE COLLEGE CHARTER.

WITH

SUNDRY ACTS AND INSTRUMENTS RELATING TO THE
POWERS AND DUTIES OF THE OVERSEERS.

CAMBRIDGE:

PRESS OF JOHN WILSON AND SON.

1877.

In Board of Overseers of Harvard College,
February 25, 1869.

Resolved. That the Rules and By-Laws of the Board of Overseers as they now stand be printed, and be bound up in the existing books of the Rules. By-Laws. Charter, and other Acts and Instruments relating to the powers and duties of the Overseers, in place of the Rules and By-Laws and their Amendments now in such books. being the first eighteen pages of said books, and the Amendments to the same.

Attest:

NATHANIEL B. SHURTLEFF,
Secretary.

Note. This edition of the Rules and By-Laws of the Board of Overseers is printed in accordance with votes passed July 12, 1876, and November 29, 1876.

Attest:

ALEXANDER McKENZIE,
Secretary.

RULES AND BY-LAWS

OF THE

OVERSEERS OF HARVARD COLLEGE.

OFFICERS.

SECTION 1. — The officers of the Board shall be a President and Secretary.

SECT. 2. — The President shall be elected by ballot, at each annual meeting; and shall hold his office for one year, and until his successor is chosen, if he so long continues a member of the Board. When a vacancy exists at any other time, it shall be filled for the remainder of the term. In the absence of the President, a president *pro tempore* shall be chosen by ballot.

SECT. 3. — The Secretary, who may or may not be a member of the Board, shall be elected by ballot at the annual meeting in the year 1868, and every third year thereafter, and shall hold his office for the term of three years, and until his successor is elected and qualified. When a vacancy occurs at any other time, it shall be filled by election for the remainder of the term. In the absence of the Secretary, a secretary *pro tempore* shall be chosen.

MEETINGS.

SECTION 4. — The annual meeting of the Overseers shall be held in Boston, on the second Wednesday of July. The other stated meetings shall be held at Cambridge on Commencement Day, and at Boston on the second Wednesdays of January, April, and October in each year, at some central place to be selected by the Secretary, unless designated by the Board. Special meetings will be convened upon application made to the Secretary, in writing, by the President of the Board, by the President or President and Fellows of the College, or by seven or more Overseers, setting forth the object of the meeting, its time and its place, either in Cambridge or Boston. Meetings may be held by adjournment at such times and places as the Board shall order.

SECT. 5. — Notice of all meetings of the Board, and of all adjournments thereof, shall be given by the Secretary, or, in case of his absence, inability, or neglect, or of a vacancy in the office, by the President: the notification of the meeting to specify its time and place, and, if a special one, its object; and to be mailed to the address of each member at least seven days, and published in not less than two newspapers of Boston at least three days, before the time of the meeting. *Provided*, that in the case of a special meeting, alleged in the application therefor to be one of great urgency, notice will be sufficient if mailed four days before the same. *And provided further*, that the Board may, in adjourning from day to day, dispense with notice thereof by the Secretary.

SECT. 6. — The votes and proceedings of the Overseers, with the names of the members present at each meeting, shall be recorded ; and the record shall be produced by the Secretary at the Overseers' meetings. At the opening of every meeting, the journal of the preceding meeting shall be read by the Secretary, unless otherwise ordered.

SECT. 7. — The Secretary shall have a list of the Overseers, ready to be produced at any meeting. He shall also acquaint the presiding officer, in writing, what Committees have not reported, and what business is by assignment to come before the Board.

SECT. 8. — A quorum of not less than nine members shall be requisite for the transaction of any business, except adjourning, or obtaining the attendance of members.

SECT. 9. — There shall be laid before the Overseers, as soon as may be after the close of the fiscal year, by the President of the University, a statement, authenticated by the Treasurer, of the expenses of the Institution during the past college year.

SECT. 10. — There shall always be presented

an attested copy of such votes of the Corporation as are laid before the Overseers for their confirmation; and the Secretary shall, from time to time, and as soon as conveniently may be, deliver to the President of the University an attested copy of the votes of the Overseers, to be by him communicated to the Corporation.

Sect. 11. — The Overseers will not receive any votes from the Corporation as to giving degrees on Commencement Day, except such as shall be presented before ten o'clock in the forenoon of that day; and the grounds and reasons of the Corporation for conferring occasional degrees shall be laid before the Overseers.

Sect. 12. — When the consent of the Overseers shall be asked to a vote of the Corporation electing any person to be an officer of instruction or government or a lecturer in the University, or conferring on any person an honorary degree, the decision shall be by ballot; except in the case of Proctors, when the question may be taken orally or by resolution.

Sect. 13. — No nomination of a member of the Corporation or of a permanent Professor shall be ratified by the Board, except at a meeting or adjournment held on seven days' notice ; nor shall any such nomination be finally acted on at the meeting or adjournment at which it shall have been made.

Sect. 14. — All Committees shall be nominated by the presiding officer, excepting in those cases where it may be otherwise determined by the Overseers ; and the person first named shall be chairman.

Sect. 15. — When any member shall require a question to be determined by yeas and nays, the President shall take the sense of the Board in that manner, provided that one fourth part of the members present shall be in favor of it.

Sect. 16. — Whenever a question shall be taken by yeas and nays, the Secretary shall call the names of all the members, except the President ; and no member shall be permitted to vote after the decision is announced from the chair.

SECT. 17. — No member shall speak more than once on one question, to the prevention of any other who has not spoken, and is desirous to speak ; nor more than twice, without leave of the Board.

SECT. 18. — When two or more members rise at once, the President shall name the member who is to speak first.

SECT. 19. — Every member, when he speaks, shall stand in his place, and address the presiding officer as " Mr. President," and shall confine himself to the question under debate.

SECT. 20. — No member speaking shall be interrupted by another, but by rising to call to order.

SECT. 21. — After a question is put to vote, no member shall speak to it.

SECT. 22. — Every motion shall be received and considered, and shall be reduced to writing if the President direct it ; and no member shall be permitted to lay a motion in writing on the table, until he has read it in his place.

Sect. 23. — A question containing two or more propositions capable of division shall be divided, whenever desired by any member.

Sect. 24. — If any member shall rise to doubt a vote upon its being declared from the chair, the President shall ascertain the number voting in the affirmative and in the negative, without any further debate. He may vote on all questions; but shall not be required to do so, unless the Board shall be equally divided, or unless his vote, if given in the minority, would affect the result.

Sect. 25. — When a vote has passed, it shall be in order for any member to move a reconsideration on the same day; and, when a motion for reconsideration is decided, that decision shall not be reconsidered.

Sect. 26. — The rules of parliamentary proceeding, as received and practised in the Legislature of this Commonwealth, shall govern the Board in all cases to which they are applicable, and in which they are not inconsistent with these Rules and By-Laws.

COMMITTEES.

SECTION 27. — There shall be the following Committees, — the first to consist wholly of *ex officio* members ; the others to be appointed at the annual meeting, or at some subsequent meeting, in such manner as the Board may determine : —

1. — A Committee to visit the University, to consist of the President and Secretary of this Board, the Governor and Lieutenant-Governor of the Commonwealth, the President of the Senate, the Speaker of the House of Representatives, the Secretary of the Board of Education, and the Chairman of each of the other Visiting Committees. This Committee will be expected to attend the annual Commencement and other public exercises of the University, or any of its departments, and to represent this Board and the Commonwealth thereat ; the President of the College, or some other officer charged with the duty, giving the members of said Committee due notice of such occasions.

2. — A Committee to visit the Academical Department, or College proper, to consist of at least nine members, six of whom shall be elective members of this Board. The duty of this Committee shall be to learn what are the methods of government and instruction in the Academical Department, to make themselves personally acquainted with the mode in which the daily recitations and private and public examina-

tions are conducted, and, in general, to take such measures, and distribute the work in such manner, as in their judgment will best enable them to report in full on the condition, wants, and prospects of the institution.

3. — A Committee to visit the Divinity School.

4. — A Committee to visit the Law School.

5. — A Committee to visit the Lawrence Scientific School and the Bussey Institution, the Peabody Museum of American Archæology and Ethnology, and the Museum of Comparative Zoölogy.

6. — A Committee to visit the Medical School and the Dental School.

7. — A Committee to visit the Observatory.

8. — A Committee to visit the Library, five of whom shall be members of this Board.

9. — A Committee to examine the Treasurer's accounts, of whom at least three shall be elective members of this Board.

10. — A Committee on Elections, to consist of five elective members of this Board, whose duty is assigned in Section 38 of these rules and by-laws.

11. — A Committee on Reports and Resolutions, to consist of seven elective members of this Board : whose duty shall be to receive the annual reports of the several Committees, after they have been read before this Board, and consider and report whether any and, if any, what action is called for by the same ; and also to attend to any other business that may be referred to them, from time to time, by this Board, and to report thereon.

SECT. 28. — Each elective member of this Board shall be upon one or more of the above-mentioned Committees. Each Visiting Committee shall consist of seven or more members, the chairman of which shall be an elective member of this Board. But persons not Overseers may be appointed to serve on any of the Visiting Committees, or on the Committee to examine the Treasurer's accounts, if specially qualified for the duty ; the same not to interfere with any express provision elsewhere made. The chairman of each of the Committees, except the Committee to visit the University, shall notify each member of the Committee, not an Overseer, of his election, with a request that he serve; and in case of his failure to accept, or of any vacancy in any such place, the Committee shall fill the same.

SECT. 29. — The apparatus, libraries, and scientific collections belonging to the several departments of the University shall be examined and reported on by the Committees appointed to visit said departments respectively.

SECT. 30. — The several Visiting Committees, except that appointed to visit the University, shall report in writing at the stated meeting in October; and their reports, after they have been read before the Board, shall be referred to the Committee on Reports and Resolutions.

SECT. 31. — After the report of the last-mentioned Committee is received and acted on by this Board, a certified copy of the record of said action, together with the reports on which it is founded, shall be referred to the Corporation.

ELECTIONS.

SECTION 32. — The election of Overseers on Commencement Day in each year, shall be held in some suitable room within the College yard, in Cambridge; notice of the time and place of which, and of the hours during which the polls will be kept open, and of the number of Overseers to be elected, including the vacancies to be filled, with the terms for which they are to be chosen, shall be given by the President and Secretary, by publication in two newspapers printed in the city of Boston, the first publication to be two weeks before the day of election.

SECT. 33. — At some meeting before each election, there shall be appointed by the Board, upon nomination by the President, one principal and two assistant inspectors of polls, who, before entering upon their duties, shall be sworn to the faithful discharge thereof.

SECT. 34. — The President and Secretary shall issue a warrant under their hands to the persons appointed inspectors of polls; specifying the number of Overseers to be elected, including the vacancies to be filled, with the terms for which they are to be chosen, and directing said inspectors to conduct the election in manner and form as the law provides, with such other instructions as to their duties as may be deemed proper: and shall furnish said inspectors with a record book and a complete list of the persons qualified to vote, to be used as a check list.

SECT. 35. — The inspectors shall carefully preserve all the ballots cast. and, after making their record thereof. shall cause the same to be sealed up in an envelope, which shall be indorsed with a certificate, under their hands, that the same contains all the ballots cast at the election for the officers therein specified, and none other. Immediately after the election, they shall deliver such envelope, so sealed and indorsed, with said record book, upon which they shall have entered their records, and said check list, to the Secretary of the Board.

SECT. 36. — The Secretary shall forthwith notify the persons who appear by the records of the inspectors to be elected ; and such persons shall be entitled to their seats as members, except as provided in the following section, and subject to the decision of the Board upon their right to hold the same.

SECT. 37. — When a person is elected to fill a vacancy, he shall not be entitled to hold his seat until the Board shall have decided his right thereto, if the person in whose place he was elected appears and claims the same.

SECT. 38. — The records and papers of the inspectors of polls shall be laid before the Board at the next assembling thereof after the election, and the same shall be referred to the Committee on Elections for their examination and report; but they need not examine the ballots returned, unless specially directed so to do by the Board.

ALTERATION AND SUSPENSION OF RULES.

SECTION 39. — Any rule or by-law may be altered or suspended by the vote of a majority of the members of the Board at the annual or other stated meeting thereof, or at any special meeting called with notice of a proposal to alter or suspend the same; and may be altered or suspended by a vote of two-thirds of the members of the Board, and may be suspended by the unanimous consent of the members present and voting; except the 13th section, which shall never be suspended, and shall never be altered or repealed, except at a meeting held at least seven days after the day on which the alteration or repeal is proposed.

CHARTER AND LAWS.

CHARTER AND LAWS.

I.

THE ACT ESTABLISHING THE OVERSEERS OF HARVARD COLLEGE.

At a General Court held at Boston, on the 8th of September, in the year 1642.

WHEREAS, through the good hand of God upon us, there is a College founded in Cambridge, in the County of Middlesex, called HARVARD COLLEGE, for the encouragement whereof this Court has given the sum of four hundred pounds, and also the revenue of the ferry betwixt Charlestown and Boston, and that the well ordering and managing of the said College is of great concernment, —

It is therefore ordered by this Court and the authority thereof, that the Governor and

Deputy-Governor for the time being, and all the magistrates of this jurisdiction, together with the teaching elders of the six next adjoining towns, — viz., Cambridge, Watertown, Charlestown, Boston, Roxbury, and Dorchester, — and the President of the said College for the time being, shall, from time to time, have full power and authority to make and establish all such orders, statutes, and constitutions as they shall see necessary for the instituting, guiding, and furthering of the said College, and the several members thereof, from time to time, in piety, morality, and learning; as also to dispose, order, and manage, to the use and behoof of the said College and the members thereof, all gifts, legacies, bequeaths, revenues, lands, and donations, as either have been, are, or shall be conferred, bestowed, or any ways shall fall or come to the said College.

And whereas it may come to pass that many of the said magistrates and elders may be absent, or otherwise employed in other weighty affairs, when the said College may need their present help and counsel, — It is therefore ordered, that the greater number of magistrates and elders which shall be present, with the President, shall have the power of the whole. *Provided*, that if any constitution, order, or orders, by them made, shall be found hurtful unto the said College, or the members thereof, or to the weal public, then, upon appeal of the party or parties grieved unto the company of Overseers first mentioned, they shall repeal the said order or orders, if they shall see cause, at their next meeting, or stand accountable thereof to the next General Court.

[This act is copied from " The General Laws of the Massachusetts Colony, revised and published by order of the General Court in October, 1658 ;" which was the second edition of the Laws of the Colony, and was printed in 1660. It varies slightly in phraseology from the Act contained in the Records of the General Court, vol. ii. page 24.]

II.

THE CHARTER OF THE PRESIDENT AND FELLOWS
OF HARVARD COLLEGE, UNDER THE SEAL OF
THE COLONY OF MASSACHUSETTS BAY, AND
BEARING DATE MAY 31, A.D. 1650.

WHEREAS, through the good hand of God,
many well-devoted persons have been, and
daily are, moved and stirred up to give and
bestow sundry gifts, legacies, lands, and revenues, for the advancement of all good literature, arts, and sciences, in HARVARD COLLEGE,
in Cambridge, in the County of Middlesex,
and to the maintenance of the President and
Fellows, and for all accommodations of buildings, and all other necessary provisions that
may conduce to the education of the English
and Indian youth of this country in knowl-
edge and godliness, —

It is therefore ordered and enacted by this
Court and the authority thereof, that for the
furthering of so good a work, and for the pur-

poses aforesaid, from henceforth that the said College in Cambridge, in Middlesex, in New England, shall be a Corporation, consisting of seven persons, to wit, a President, five Fellows, and a Treasurer or Bursar ; and that HENRY DUNSTER shall be the first President, SAMUEL MATHER, SAMUEL DANFORTH, Masters of Art, JONATHAN MITCHELL, COMFORT STARR, and SAMUEL EATON, Bachelors of Art, shall be the five Fellows, and THOMAS DANFORTH to be present Treasurer, all of them being inhabitants in the Bay, and shall be the first seven persons of which the said Corporation shall consist ; and that the said seven persons, or the greater number of them, procuring the presence of the Overseers of the College, and by their counsel and consent, shall have power, and are hereby authorized, at any time or times, to elect a new President, Fellows, or Treasurer, so oft, and from time to time, as any of the said person or persons shall die or be removed ; which said

President and Fellows for the time being shall for ever hereafter, in name and fact, be one body politic and corporate in law, to all intents and purposes, and shall have perpetual ·succession, and shall be called by the name of *President and Fellows of Harvard College*, and shall from time to time be eligible as aforesaid ; and, by that name, they and their successors shall and may purchase and acquire to themselves, or take and receive upon free gift and donation, any lands, tenements, or hereditaments, within this jurisdiction of the Massachusetts, not exceeding the value of five hundred pounds per annum, and any goods and sums of money whatsoever to the use and behoof of the said President, Fellows, and scholars of the said College; and also may sue and plead. or be sued and impleaded, by the name aforesaid, in all courts and places of judicature within the jurisdiction aforesaid.

And that the said President, with any

three of the Fellows, shall have power, and are hereby authorized, when they shall think fit, to make and appoint a common seal for the use of the said Corporation. And the President and Fellows, or the major part of them, from time to time, may meet and choose such officers and servants for the College, and make such allowance to them, and them also to remove, and, after death or removal, to choose such others, and to make from time to time such orders and by-laws, for the better ordering and carrying-on the work of the College, as they shall think fit; *provided* the said orders be allowed by the Overseers. And also that the President and Fellows, or major part of them, with the Treasurer, shall have power to make conclusive bargains for lands and tenements, to be purchased by the said Corporation for valuable considerations.

And, for the better ordering of the government of the said College and Corporation, — Be it enacted by the authority aforesaid, that the President and three more of the Fellows shall and may from time to time, upon due warning or notice given by the President to the rest, hold a meeting for the debating and concluding of affairs concerning the profits and revenues of any lands, and disposing of their goods (provided that all the said disposings be according to the will of the donors), and for direction in all emergent occasions, execution of all orders and by-laws, and for the procuring of a general meeting of all the Overseers and Society in great and difficult cases, and in cases of non-agreement; in all which cases aforesaid, the conclusion shall be made by the major part, the said President having a casting voice, the Overseers consenting thereunto. And that all the aforesaid transactions shall tend to and for the use and behoof of the President, Fellows, scholars, and officers of the said College, and for all accommodations of buildings, books, and all other necessary provisions and furnitures as may be for the advancement and education of youth in all manner of good literature, arts, and sciences.

And, further, be it ordered by this Court and the authority thereof, that all the lands, tenements, or hereditaments, houses, or revenues, within this jurisdiction, to the aforesaid President or College appertaining, not exceeding the value of five hundred pounds per annum, shall from henceforth be freed from all civil impositions, taxes, and rates ; all goods to the said Corporation, or to any scholars thereof, appertaining, shall be exempted from all manner of toll, customs, and excise whatsoever ; and that the said President, Fellows, and scholars, together with the servants, and other necessary officers to the said President or College appertaining, not exceeding ten, — viz., three to the President and seven to the College belonging, — shall be exempted from all personal civil offices, military exercises or services, watchings and wardings; and such of their estates, not exceeding one hundred pounds a man, shall be free from all country taxes or rates whatsoever, and none others.

In witness whereof, the Court hath caused the seal of the Colony to be hereunto affixed. Dated the one and thirtieth day of the third month, called May, anno 1650.

[L. S.]   THO: DUDLEY, *Governor*.

[The above is a copy of the original Charter engrossed on parchment, under the signature of Gov. Dudley, with the Colony seal appendant, in the custody of the President and Fellows of Harvard College. The Charter, varying slightly in phraseology, is also contained in the Records of the General Court, vol. iv. page 10.]

III.

AN APPENDIX TO THE COLLEGE CHARTER, GRANTED BY AN ACT OF THE GENERAL COURT OF THE COLONY PASSED A.D. 1657.

At a General Court held at Boston, the 14th of October, 1657.

IN answer to certain proposals presented to this Court by the Overseers of HARVARD

COLLEGE, as an appendix to the College Charter, it is ordered, —

The Corporation shall have power, from time to time, to make such orders and by-laws, for the better ordering and carrying-on of the work of the College, as they shall see cause, without dependence upon the consent of the Overseers foregoing. *Provided always*, that the Corporation shall be responsible unto, and those orders and by-laws shall be alterable by, the Overseers, according to their discretion.

And when the Corporation shall hold a meeting, and agreeing with College servants, for making of orders and by-laws, for debating and concluding of affairs concerning the profits and revenues of any lands or gifts, and the disposing thereof (provided that all the said disposals be according to the will of the donors), for managing of all emergent occasions, for the procuring of a general meeting of the Overseers and Society in great and difficult cases. and in cases of non-agreement, and for all other College affairs to them pertaining. — in all these cases the conclusion shall be valid, being made by the major part of the Corporation. the President having a casting vote. *Provided always*, that, in these things also. they be responsible to the Overseers as aforesaid.

And in case the Corporation shall see cause to call a meeting of the Overseers, or the Overseers shall think good to meet of themselves. it shall be sufficient unto the validity of College acts. that notice be given to the Overseers in the six towns mentioned in the printed law. anno 1642. when the rest of the Overseers, by reason of the remoteness of their habitations, cannot conveniently be acquainted therewith.

[This Act is taken from the Records of the General Court. vol. iv. page 265.]

IV.

EXTRACT FROM A RESOLVE OF THE PROVINCIAL
GENERAL COURT, PASSED A.D. 1707, DECLAR-
ING THE COLLEGE CHARTER OF 1650 NOT
REPEALED, AND DIRECTING THE PRESIDENT AND
FELLOWS OF THE COLLEGE TO EXERCISE THE
POWERS GRANTED BY IT.

*At a Great and General Court for her Majesty's
Province of the Massachusetts Bay, begun and
held at Boston upon the 28th of May, 1707, and
continued by several prorogations unto the 29th of
October following, being the third session.*

IN COUNCIL.

Thursday, Dec. 4, 1707.

AND inasmuch as the first foundation and
establishment of that House [Harvard College, in Cambridge], and the government
thereof, had its original from an act of the
General Court, made and passed in the year
1650, which has not been repealed or nulled,

—the President and Fellows of the said College are directed, from time to time, to regulate themselves according to the rules of the Constitution by the said Act prescribed, and to exercise the powers and authorities thereby granted for the government of that House, and the support thereof.

Saturday, Dec. 6, 1707.

The Representatives returned the Vote passed in Council, the 4th current, referring to the College, with their concurrence thereunto.

By his Excellency the Governor, consented to,

JOSEPH DUDLEY.

[This Resolve is taken from the Records of the General Court, vol. viii., page 344.]

V.

THE ARTICLES OF THE CONSTITUTION OF THE COMMONWEALTH OF MASSACHUSETTS, CONFIRMING AND SECURING TO HARVARD COLLEGE THE PERPETUAL POSSESSION AND ENJOYMENT OF ALL ITS ESTATES, RIGHTS, POWERS, AND PRIVILEGES.

CHAPTER V.

SECT. I. — *The University.*

ARTICLE 1. — Whereas our wise and pious ancestors, so early as the year one thousand six hundred and thirty-six, laid the foundation of HARVARD COLLEGE, in which University many persons of great eminence have, by the blessing of God, been initiated in those arts and sciences which qualified them for public employments both in Church and State ; and whereas the encouragement of arts and sciences and all good literature tends to the honor of God, the advantage of the Christian religion, and the great benefit of this and the other United States of America, — It is declared that the *President and Fellows of Harvard College* in their corporate capacity, and their successors in that capacity, their officers and servants, shall have, hold, use, exercise, and enjoy all the powers, authorities, rights, liberties, privileges, immunities, and franchises which they now have, or are entitled to have, hold, use, exercise, and enjoy; and the same are hereby ratified and confirmed unto them, the said President and Fellows of Harvard College, and to their successors, and to their officers and servants respectively, for ever.

ART. 2. — And whereas there have been at sundry times, by divers persons, gifts, grants, devises of houses, lands, tenements, goods, chattels, legacies, and conveyances, heretofore made either to Harvard College, in Cambridge, in New England, or to the President and Fellows of Harvard College, or to the said College by some other description, under several charters successively, — It is declared that all the said gifts, grants, devises, legacies, and conveyances are hereby for ever confirmed unto the President and Fellows of Harvard College, and to their successors in the capacity aforesaid, according to the true intent and meaning of the donor or donors, grantor or grantors, devisor or devisors.

ART. 3. — And whereas, by an Act of the General Court of the Colony of Massachusetts Bay, passed in the year one thousand six hundred and forty-two, the Governor and Deputy-Governor for the time being, and all the magistrates of that jurisdiction, were with the President, and a number of the clergy in the said Act described, constituted the Overseers of Harvard College ; and it being necessary, in this new constitution of government, to ascertain who shall be deemed successors to the said Governor, Deputy-Governor, and magistrates, — It is declared that the Governor, Lieutenant-Governor,

Council, and Senate of this Commonwealth are and shall be deemed their successors; who with the President of Harvard College for the time being, together with the ministers of the Congregational churches in the towns of Cambridge, Watertown, Charlestown, Boston, Roxbury, and Dorchester, mentioned in the said Act, shall be, and hereby are, vested with all the powers and authority belonging or in any way appertaining to the Overseers of Harvard College. *Provided,* that nothing herein shall be construed to prevent the Legislature of this Commonwealth from making such alterations in the government of the said University as shall be conducive to its advantage, and the interest of the republic of letters, in as full a manner as might have been done by the Legislature of the late Province of the Massachusetts Bay.

VI.

AN ACT TO ALTER AND AMEND THE CONSTI-
TUTION OF THE BOARD OF OVERSEERS OF
HARVARD COLLEGE.

WHEREAS the members of the Board of
Overseers of Harvard College, as heretofore
constituted, cannot conveniently nor con-
stantly attend to the diligent discharge of the
duties enjoined on it : —

SECTION 1. — The Governor, Lieutenant-
Governor, Counsellors, President of the Senate, and Speaker of the House of Representatives of the Commonwealth, and the
President of Harvard College for the time
being, with fifteen ministers of Congregational
churches and fifteen laymen, all inhabitants
within the State, to be elected as is hereafter
mentioned, shall for ever hereafter constitute
the Board of Overseers of Harvard College ;
they, or the major part of them present at
any legal meeting, to exercise and enjoy all

the rights, powers, and privileges, and to be subject to all the duties, of the existing Board of Overseers of Harvard College. *Provided, however,* that all the ministers of Congregational churches who are members of that Board shall remain members of the Board of Overseers established by this Act, so long as they shall continue ministers respectively of their Congregational churches, and no longer.

[Sect. 2. — As soon as conveniently may be after this Act shall be in force, the present Secretary of the Board of Overseers, or, if that office be vacant, the President or a major part of the Fellows of Harvard College, shall call a meeting of the Overseers of Harvard College, to be holden at some suitable time and place, for electing fifteen laymen, inhabitants of the State, to be members of the Board of Overseers; the said meeting to be notified by publishing the time and place of holding the same, in each of the public newspapers printed in Boston, ten days at the least before the time of holding the same: and the said elections to be made by ballot, by the major part of the Overseers present: and all persons who then, if this Act had not been in force, would have been members of the Board of Overseers of Harvard College, shall have right to meet and vote in the said elections.]

SECT. 3. — The Board of Overseers, as constituted by this Act, may, at any legal meeting, choose by a majority of votes a Secretary, when that office shall be vacant, who shall be under oath truly to record all the votes and proceedings of the Board, and faithfully to discharge all the duties of his office ; and the said Board may at any legal meeting, by a majority of votes, determine from time to time when and in what manner its meetings shall be held, called, and notified: [and, at any legal meeting of the said Board, the Governor, if present, shall preside; if not, the Lieutenant-Governor, if present, shall preside; in their absence, the oldest member of the Council present shall preside ; if they also be absent, the President of the Senate shall preside, if present; but, in his absence also, the Speaker of the House of Representatives shall preside ; and, if neither of them be present, the greater part of the Overseers present at such meeting shall choose a president *pro tempore*, and until one of the officers aforesaid shall be present.] *Provided, nevertheless*, that the Secretary of the Overseers shall have power to call a meeting of the said Board, at such times as he shall be thereto requested by the President and Fellows of Harvard College ; such meeting to be notified as the said Board shall direct.

SECT. 4. — [When any minister of any Congregational church, being a member of the said Board, shall cease to have the ministerial relation he now has, or may have had at the time of his election, or,] when any member of the elective part of the said Board shall remove out of the State, the place of such [minister or] member shall thereupon become vacant. And the said Board may at any legal meeting, by a vote of the greater number present, remove from his place any member of the elective part of the said Board who shall neglect to attend the meetings thereof, without reasonable excuse, when duly notified, or who by his immoral conduct shall have rendered himself unworthy of holding his place ; but, before any vote shall pass to remove any member, he shall have reasonable notice, and a fit opportunity to be heard in his defence.

[SECT. 5. —For establishing a perpetual succession in the elective part of the said Board, whenever a vacancy shall happen therein, by death, resignation, or otherwise, the Overseers may, at a legal meeting, by a majority of the votes present, fill up such vacancy by electing therefor some suitable person, who shall be an inhabitant of the State. *Provided, however*, that no minister of any Congregational church shall be so elected when there are fifteen ministers of Congregational churches members of the elective part of the said Board, nor shall any laymen be so elected when there are fifteen laymen members of the elective part of the said Board; but, in all cases when there are fifteen ministers and fifteen laymen members of the elective part of the said Board, there shall not be deemed to be any vacancy therein.]

SECT. 6. — This Act shall be in force when the Overseers of Harvard College, as heretofore constituted, and the President and Fellows of Harvard College, shall agree to accept the provisions in this Act contained.

[March 6, 1810.]

[The provisions of this Act were accepted by the President and Fellows on the 16th of March, 1810; and by the Overseers, on the 12th of April in the same year.]

VII.

An Act to repeal an Act entitled "An Act to alter and amend the Constitution of the Overseers of Harvard College, and to regulate certain Meetings of that Board.

[Section 1. — An Act made and passed the seventh day of March, in the year of our Lord one thousand eight hundred and ten, entitled "An Act to alter and amend the Constitution of the Board of Overseers of Harvard College," be, and the same is hereby, repealed; and the Board of Overseers, from and after the passing of this Act, shall be constituted in the same way and manner, and be composed of the same persons, and no others, that it would have been had the same Act never been made or passed.

Sect. 2. — There shall be a meeting of the Board of Overseers of Harvard College, as the same will be constituted after the passing of this Act, on the second Wednesday of the first session of the General Court annually, in the Senate Chamber, at three o'clock in the afternoon (unless otherwise ordered by the said Board of Overseers), if the General Court shall remain so long in session, and at such other times and places as the said Board shall order; at which annual meeting it shall be the duty of the Secretary of said Board, at the first meeting thereof, to lay before them the records and proceedings of the Corporation of Harvard College, and of the said Board of Overseers, which have been had since the passing of the Act aforesaid, which is hereby repealed; and, in like manner, all the proceedings which may have been had by said Corporation, and Board of Overseers, shall be laid before them at their next succeeding meeting, to be held agreeably to the provisions of this Act.]   [Feb. 29, 1812.]

[This Act was not assented to by the Overseers, or by the President and Fellows; but its validity was denied by both Boards, and it was repealed by the Act on the next page.]

VIII.

AN ACT TO RESTORE THE BOARD OF OVERSEERS
OF HARVARD COLLEGE, AND TO MAKE AN ADDI-
TION THERETO.

SECTION 1. — An Act made and passed on
the twenty-eighth day of February, in the
year of our Lord one thousand eight hundred
and twelve, entitled "An Act to repeal an
Act entitled ' An Act to alter and amend the
Constitution of the Board of Overseers of
Harvard College, and to regulate certain
meetings of that Board,' " be, and the same
is hereby, repealed.

[SECT. 2. — The Senate of this Commonwealth shall
be, and they hereby are, added to the Board of Overseers constituted by an Act made and passed on the
fifth day of March, in the year of our Lord one thousand eight hundred and ten, entitled " An Act to alter
and amend the Constitution of the Board of Overseers
of Harvard College," and shall, together with the persons mentioned in the said last-mentioned Act, hereafter constitute the Board of Overseers of Harvard
College ; they, or the major part of them present at

any legal meeting, to exercise and enjoy all the rights, powers, and privileges, and to be subject to all the duties, of the Board of Overseers constituted under the said last-mentioned Act.]

SECT. 3. — This Act shall be in force when the Overseers of Harvard College, constituted by the last-mentioned Act, and the President and Fellows of Harvard College, shall agree to accept the provisions of this Act. [Feb. 28, 1814.]

[The provisions of this Act were accepted by the President and Fellows on the 10th of March, 1814 ; and by the Overseers, on the 17th of the same month.]

48 BOARD OF OVERSEERS.

IX.

AN ACT IN ADDITION TO "AN ACT TO ALTER AND AMEND THE CONSTITUTION OF THE BOARD OF OVERSEERS OF HARVARD COLLEGE.

[SECTION 1.— Whenever any vacancy exists in the clerical part of the Board of Overseers of Harvard College, the Board, in filling such vacancy, agreeably to the provisions of the statute of one thousand eight hundred and nine, chapter one hundred and fourteen, may elect any stated minister of a church of Christ, ordained agreeably to the usages of the order to which he may belong. *Provided*, that when any minister so elected shall cease to have the ministerial relation he had at the time of his election, or shall remove out of the Commonwealth, the place of such minister at said Board shall thereupon become vacant.

SECT. 2. — This Act shall be in force when the Overseers of Harvard College, and the President and Fellows of Harvard College, shall accept the provisions of the same.] [March 28th, 1834.]

[The provisions of this Act were accepted by the Overseers on the 16th of February, 1843 ; and by the President and Fellows, on the 25th of the same month.]

X.

An Act to change the Organization of the Board of Overseers of the University at Cambridge.

[Section 1. — The Board of Overseers of Harvard College, as constituted by existing laws, shall continue until the day of the next annual meeting of the General Court, and no longer.]

Sect. 2. — [The Governor, Lieutenant-Governor, President of the Senate, and Speaker of the House of Representatives of the Commonwealth, the Secretary of the Board of Education, and] the President and Treasurer of Harvard College, for the time being, together with thirty other persons, as hereinafter defined and described, and no others, shall [on and after the day of the next annual meeting of the General Court] constitute the Board of Overseers of Harvard College ; they, or the major part of them present at any legal meeting, to exercise and enjoy all the rights, powers, and privileges, and to be subject to all the duties, of the existing Board of Overseers.

[SECT. 3. — The thirty persons, who, in addition to
the *ex-officio* members thereof, now constitute the
Board of Overseers, shall be divided into three classes
of ten each, by lot or otherwise, as they themselves
may determine ; and the persons of the first class shall
go out of office on the day of the next annual meeting
of the General Court, and their places be supplied
by joint ballot of the Senators and Representatives of
the Commonwealth, assembled in one room ; and the
persons of the second class shall go out of office on the
day of the annual meeting of the General Court, which
will be in the year one thousand eight hundred and
fifty-three, and their places be supplied in like manner
by joint ballot of the Senators and Representatives ;
and the persons of the third class shall go out of office
on the day of the annual meeting of the General Court
which will be in the year one thousand eight hundred
and fifty-four, and their places be supplied in like manner by joint ballot of the Senators and Representatives.
Provided, that the persons of each of the said outgoing
classes shall continue in office for two months after the
day of the said annual meeting of the General Court,
unless their successors shall have been sooner chosen
by the Senators and Representatives.]

SECT. 4. — [When the Board of Overseers shall
have been wholly renewed in the manner prescribed in
the foregoing section,] the members thereof shall
be divided into six equal classes [by subdivision
of the previous classes into two each, according to lot

or otherwise, as the Board may determine, and having regard to seniority of service among the said previous classes in arranging the order of precedence of the new series]; and the said six classes shall [thereafter] go out of office in rotation, and in order of precedence as thus defined, one at each successive annual [meeting of the General Court, and their places be supplied by joint ballot of the Senators and Representatives]. (Commencement.*)

[SECT. 5. — Any vacancy occurring in the said Board of Overseers, whether by death, resignation, removal from the Commonwealth, or otherwise, shall be filled by joint ballot of the Senators and Representatives, as hereinbefore provided ; and if the General Court shall omit to fill, within three months from the day of its annual meeting as aforesaid, any existing vacancy, then such vacancy may be filled by the remaining Overseers ; but the person so elected to fill any vacancy, whether by Senators and Representatives or by the Overseers, shall be deemed a member of, and go out of office with, the class to which his predecessor belonged.]

[SECT. 6. — The Governor, if present, shall preside at any legal meeting of said Board of Overseers ; if not, the Lieutenant-Governor; in their absence, the

* By Act of 1865, see p. 58.

President of the Senate ; in his absence, the Speaker of the House of Representatives ; but if neither of the persons named be present, then the meeting shall elect a president *pro tempore;*] and the said Board may choose by majority of votes a Secretary, when that office shall be vacant, who shall be under oath truly to record the votes and proceedings of the Board, and faithfully to discharge all the duties of his office ; and the said Board may make, establish, and alter such rules of proceeding, and other by-laws, as they shall deem meet, *provided* that the same be not inconsistent with the constitution and laws of the Commonwealth.

SECT. 7.— [No member of the General Court which elects shall be eligible to a place ·in the said Board of Overseers ; and] no person shall be re-eligible for more than one term immediately succeeding that for which he shall have been first elected.

SECT. 8. — This Act shall be in force when the Board of Overseers as heretofore constituted, and the President and Fellows of Harvard College, respectively, at meetings held for that purpose during the present session of the General Court, shall by vote have assented to the same ; *provided*, that nothing contained herein shall be deemed to prejudice any constitutional powers which may be possessed by the General Court.

SECT. 9. — All Acts, or parts of Acts, inconsistent herewith are repealed.

[May 22, 1851.]

[This Act was assented to by the President and Fellows on the 22d of May, 1851; and by the Overseers on the same day.]

XI.

An Act explanatory of the Acts relating to the Organization of the Board of Overseers of the University at Cambridge.

Section 1. — The several Acts relating to the organization of the Board of Overseers of Harvard College shall be so construed as to empower the said Board to order and provide. by rule or by-law. what number of the members thereof. not less than nine, shall constitute a quorum or legal meeting of the same.

Sect. 2. — This Act shall take effect from and after its passage.   [March 3, 1852.]

XII.

An Act in addition to the Act to change the Organization of the Board of Overseers of the University at Cambridge.

[Section 1. — All elections to fill vacancies in the Board of Overseers of Harvard College shall hereafter be by concurrent vote of the two branches of the General Court.

Sect. 2. — The members of said Board of each of the outgoing classes shall continue in office for two months after the day of the annual meeting of the General Court, notwithstanding that their successors may have been sooner chosen.

Sect. 3. — This Act shall be in force when the Board of Overseers and the President and Fellows of Harvard College, respectively, at meetings held for that purpose, prior to the first day of February next, shall by vote have assented to the same; *provided*, that nothing herein contained shall be deemed to prejudice any constitutional powers which may be possessed by the General Court.] [April 6, 1859.]

[This Act was assented to by the Overseers on the 26th of January, 1860; and by the President and Fellows on the 28th of the same month.]

XIII.

An Act in relation to the Board of Overseers of Harvard College.

SECTION 1. — The places of the successive classes in the Board of Overseers of Harvard College, and the vacancies in such classes, shall hereafter be annually supplied by ballot of such persons as have received from the College a degree of bachelor of arts, or master of arts, or any honorary degree, voting on Commencement Day in the city of Cambridge; such election to be first held in the year eighteen hundred and sixty-six: *provided, however,* that no member of the corporation, and no officer of government or instruction in said College, shall be eligible as an Overseer, or entitled to vote in the election of Overseers; and *provided, further,* that no person who has received from said College the degree of bachelor of arts shall be entitled to vote for Overseers before the fifth annual election after the graduation of his class.

SECT. 2. — The Board of Overseers shall annually appoint one principal and two or more assistant inspectors of polls, who shall, on Commencement Day, from the hour of ten in the forenoon to the hour of four in the afternoon, at some place in said city of Cambridge, fixed by said Board, receive the votes for Overseers, and they shall sort and count such votes, and make public declaration thereof, after the closing of the polls; and said inspectors shall be provided with a complete list of the persons qualified to vote at such election, and no person shall vote until the inspectors find and check his name upon such list. The names of the persons voted for, the number of votes received for each person, and the vacancy or place in said Board for which he is proposed, shall be entered in words at length, by said inspectors, upon a record kept by them for that purpose, which shall, after such election, be forthwith made up, signed, and delivered by them to the Board of Overseers. The persons who shall receive the highest number of votes for the places or vacancies in said Board shall, to the number of Overseers to be elected, be deemed and shall be declared by said Board elected to be members thereof.

SECT. 3. — The Board of Overseers shall give notice of the place of the polls, the hours during which they are open, and the number of Overseers to be elected, by publishing the same at least ten days before Commencement Day in some newspaper printed in the city of Boston.

SECT. 4. — The terms of office of the existing classes of Overseers are extended to the close of Commencement Day of the year in which such terms severally expire; the terms of office of the classes hereafter elected shall successively expire at the close of Commencement Day each year in their order; and the persons elected Overseers on any Commencement Day shall supply the places of the class of Overseers which goes out of office at the close of that day, and the vacancies then existing in said Board.

SECT. 5. — Whenever there shall be a failure on Commencement Day to supply any places or vacancies in the Board of Overseers, the same may be filled by vote of the remaining Overseers; and any person elected to fill a vacancy shall be deemed to be a member of, and to go out of office with, the class to which his predecessor belonged.

SECT. 6. — The Governor, Lieutenant-Governor, President of the Senate, Speaker of the House of Representatives, and Secretary of the Board of Education, shall not be *ex-officio* members of the Board of Overseers of Harvard College after this Act shall be in force.

SECT. 7. — This Act shall be in force when the Board of Overseers and the President

and Fellows of Harvard College respectively,
at meetings held for that purpose. shall by
vote have assented to the same.

SECT. 8. — This Act shall not be construed
as in the nature of a contract or a charter.
but may at any time be repealed at the pleas-
ure of the Legislature.   [April 28, 1865.]

[This Act was assented to by the Overseers on the
21st of September. 1865: and by the President and
Fellows, on the 15th of December of the same year.]

www.ingramcontent.com/pod-product-compliance
Lightning Source LLC
Chambersburg PA
CBHW031748090426
42739CB00008B/933